Usborne
Mosaic Sticker
Castles

Designed and illustrated by
Nayera Everall

Written by
Kirsteen Robson

There is a fold-out page at the back of the book where you can
try out ideas, or put your stickers while you are not using them.

Towers and turrets

Build a castle with your stickers.
Here are some things you can include.

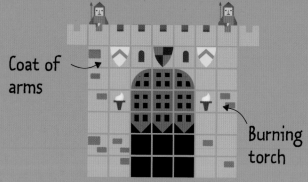

Coat of
arms

Burning
torch

The wooden portcullis in this
gatehouse is halfway up.

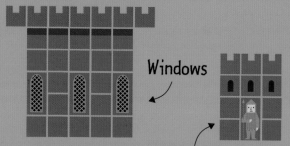

Windows

You can add this tower
above the gatehouse.

Soldier on guard

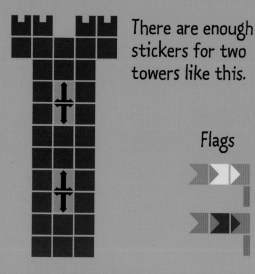

There are enough
stickers for two
towers like this.

Flags

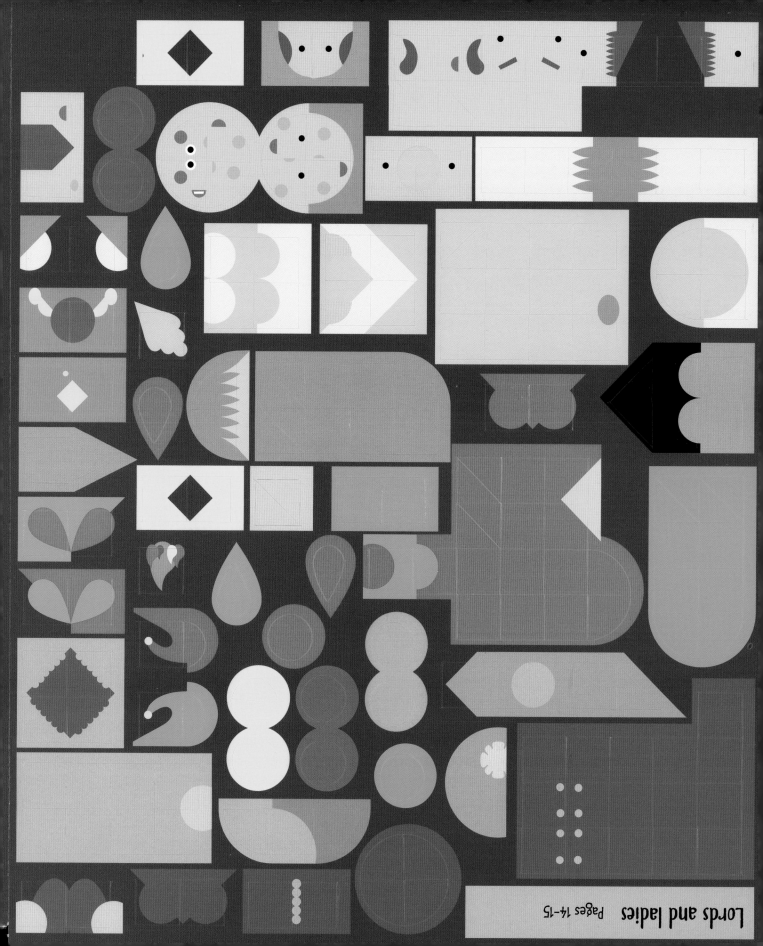

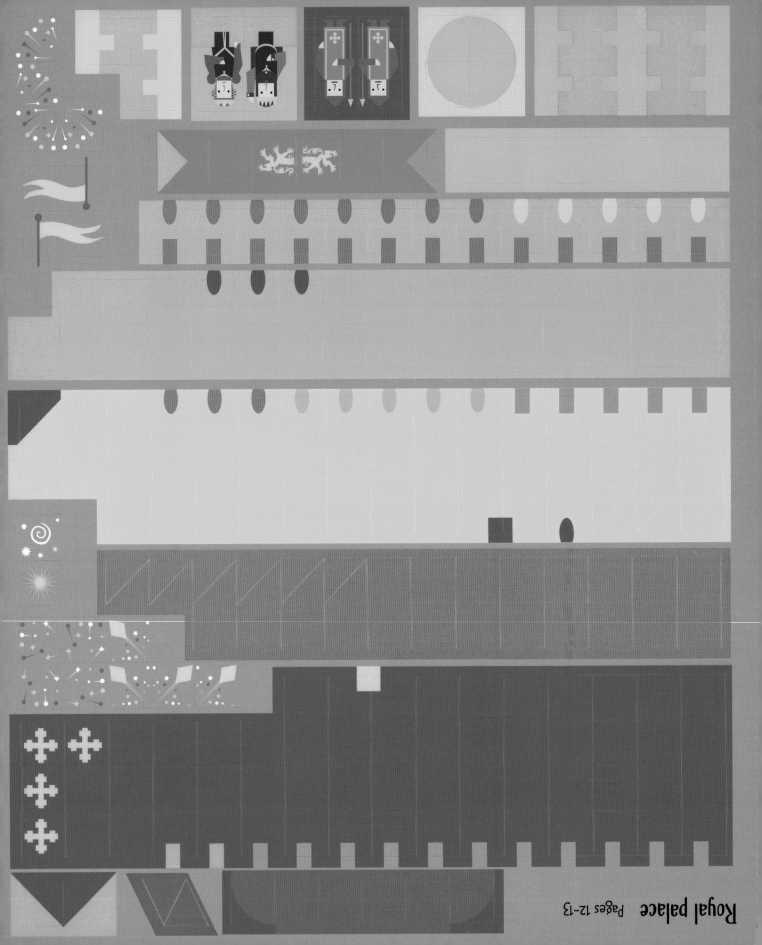

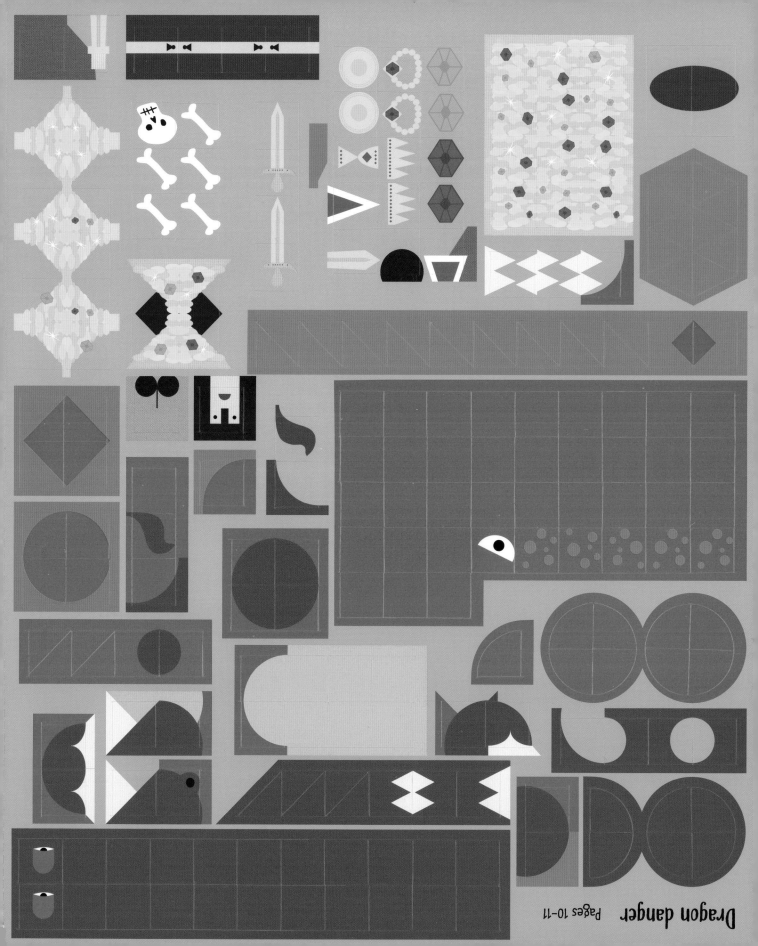

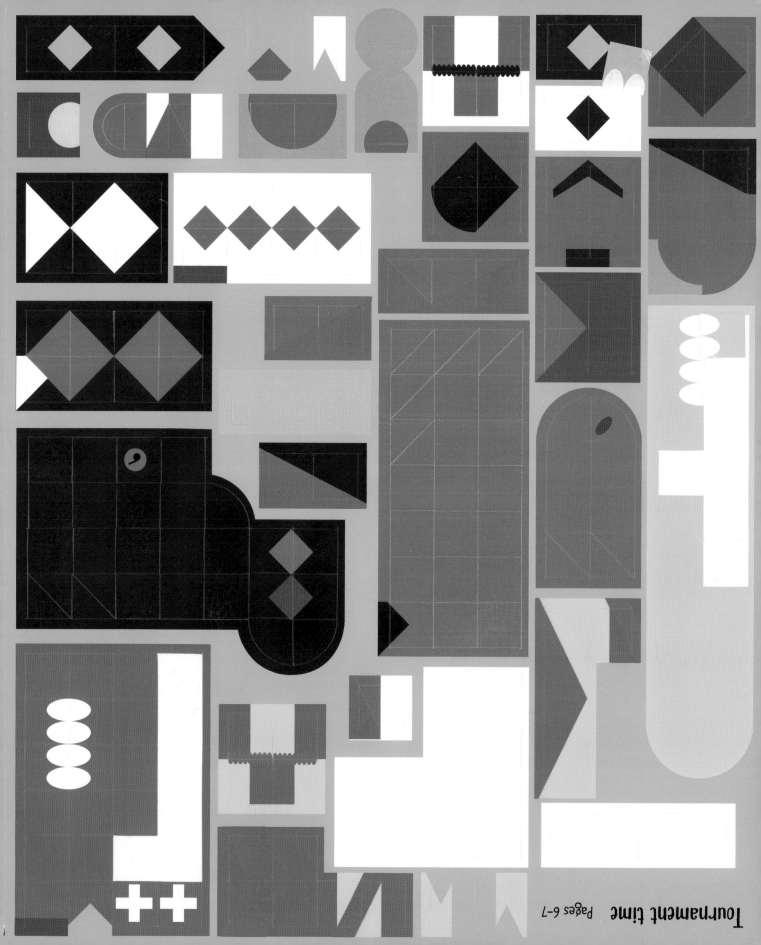

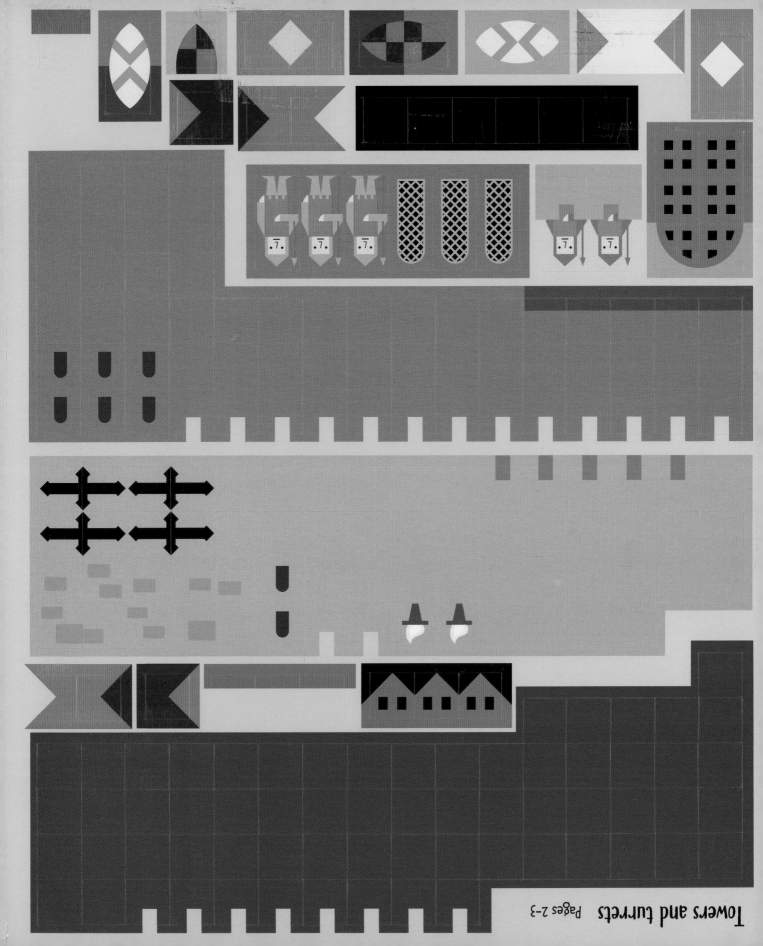

Coats of arms

Design some banners and shields. Here are some ideas to get you started.

Decorative edge

Small banners

Play around with the stickers to create different patterns.

Small shields

Useful symbols

Splendid banquet

Fill these pages with delicious dishes.
Here are some suggestions for the menu.

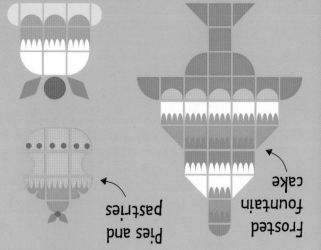

Frosted
fountain
cake

Pies and
pastries

Make these dainty desserts, or use the
stickers to create your own.

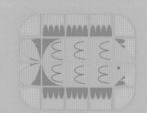

Pig's head platter

Fresh fish

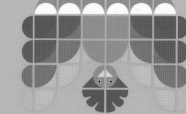

Bread rolls

Roasted pheasant

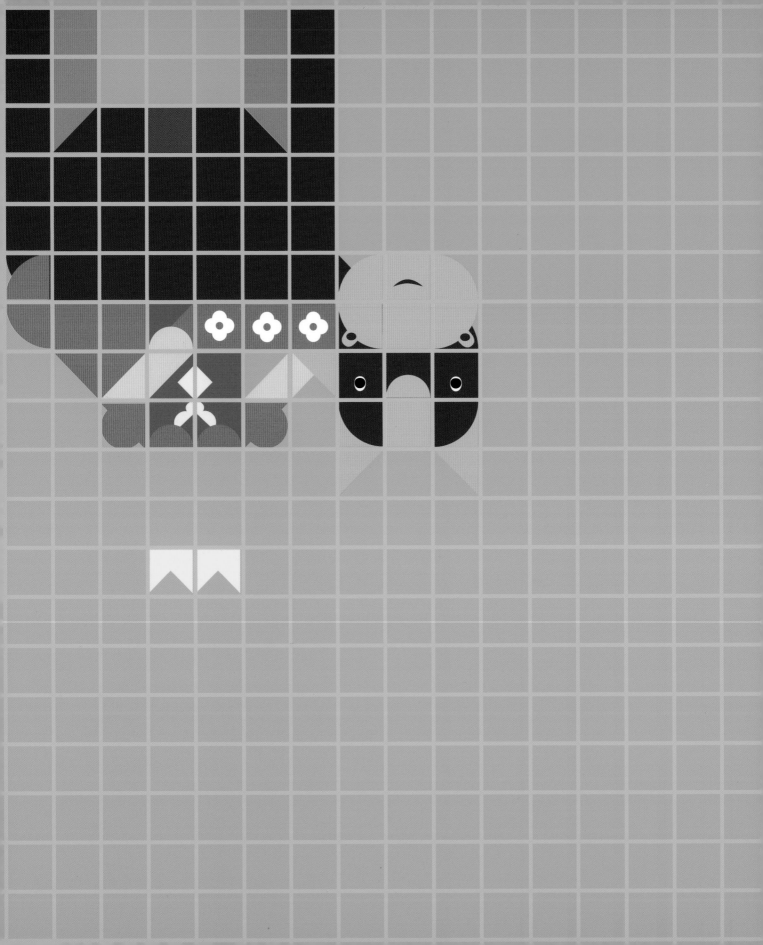

Hunting party

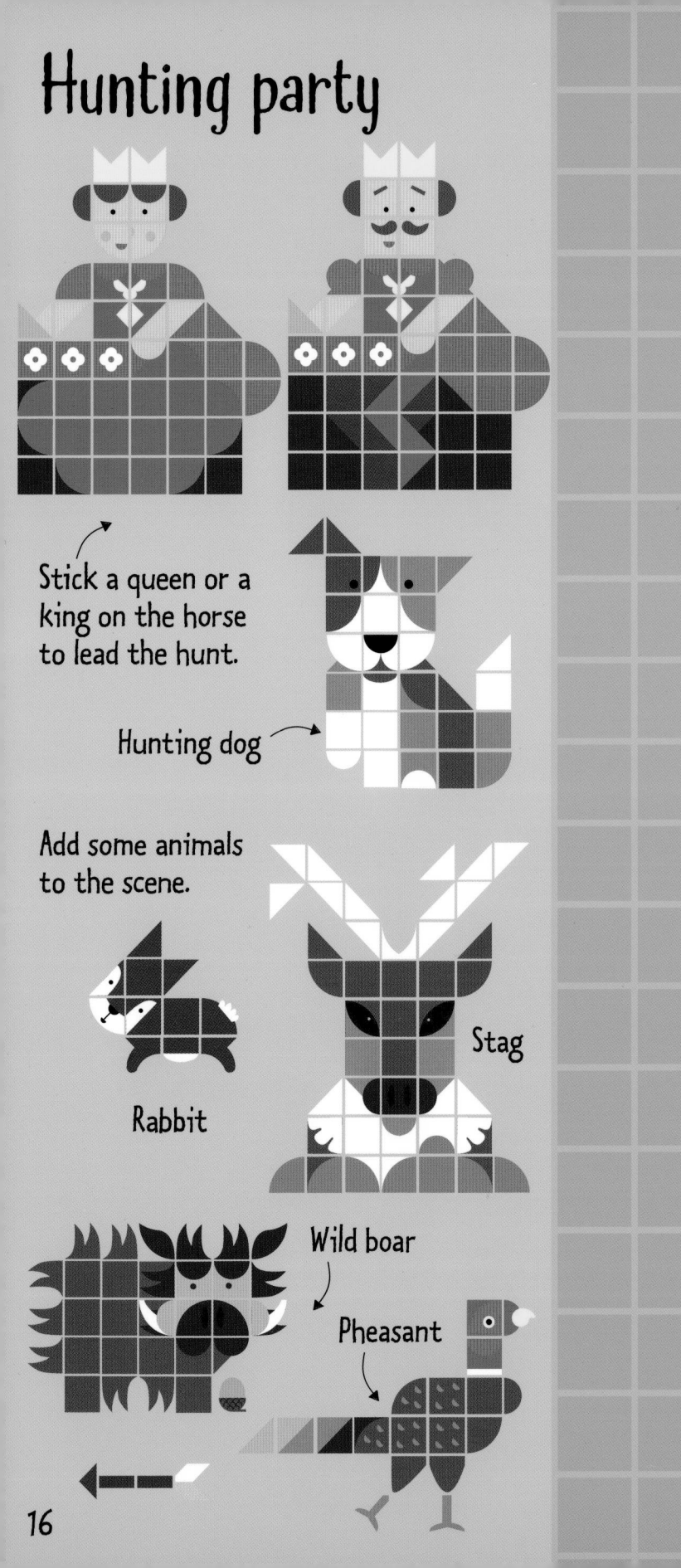

Stick a queen or a king on the horse to lead the hunt.

Hunting dog

Add some animals to the scene.

Rabbit

Stag

Wild boar

Pheasant

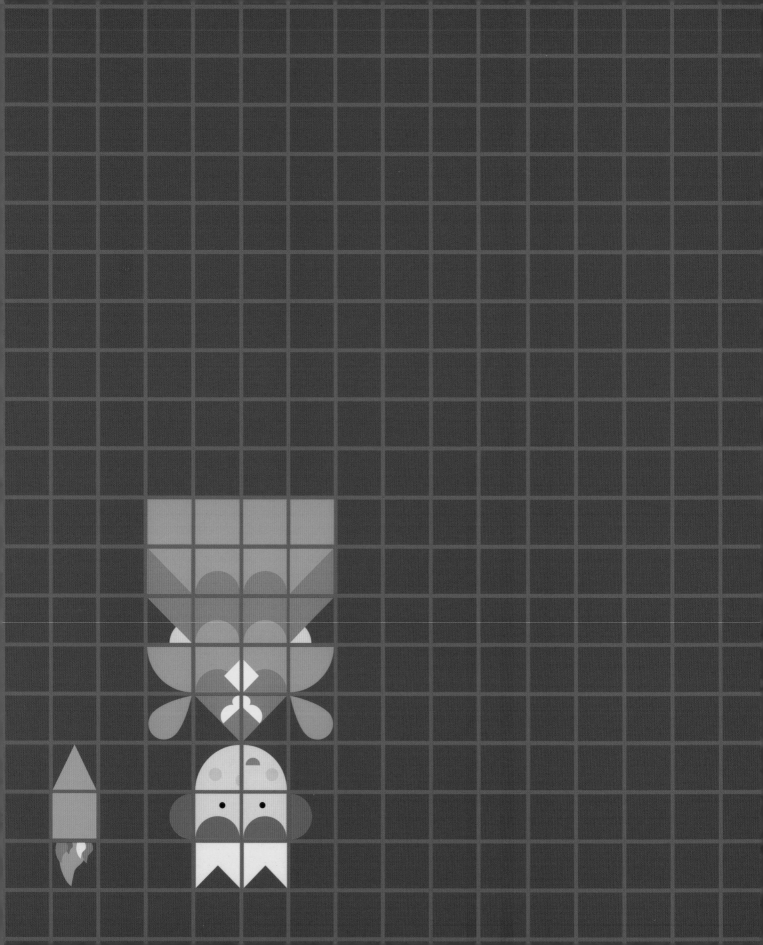

Lords and ladies

Who will be invited to the Queen's ball?

The King
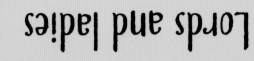

Use the ideas below to add some guests.

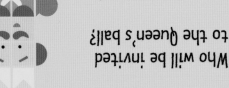

Light up the Great Hall.

Juggling jester
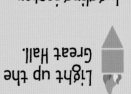

Lord and Lady Violetta
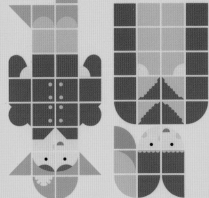

Sir Rowan and his sister, Rose
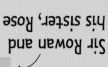
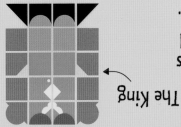

Royal palace

Here are some ideas you could put together to make a spectacular palace.

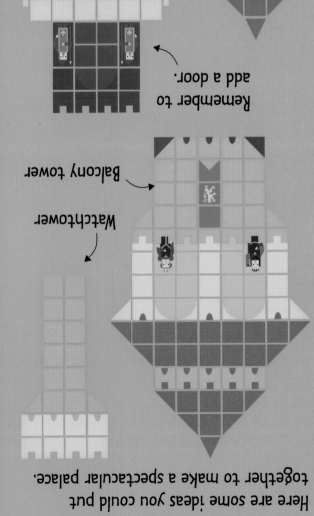

Watchtower

Balcony tower

Remember to add a door.

You could top one end of the castle walls with a tower like this.

Fireworks

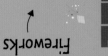

Use the stone stickers for building walls.

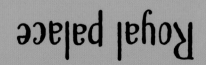

Dragon danger

Copy the dragons' bodies below, then mix and match the other features.

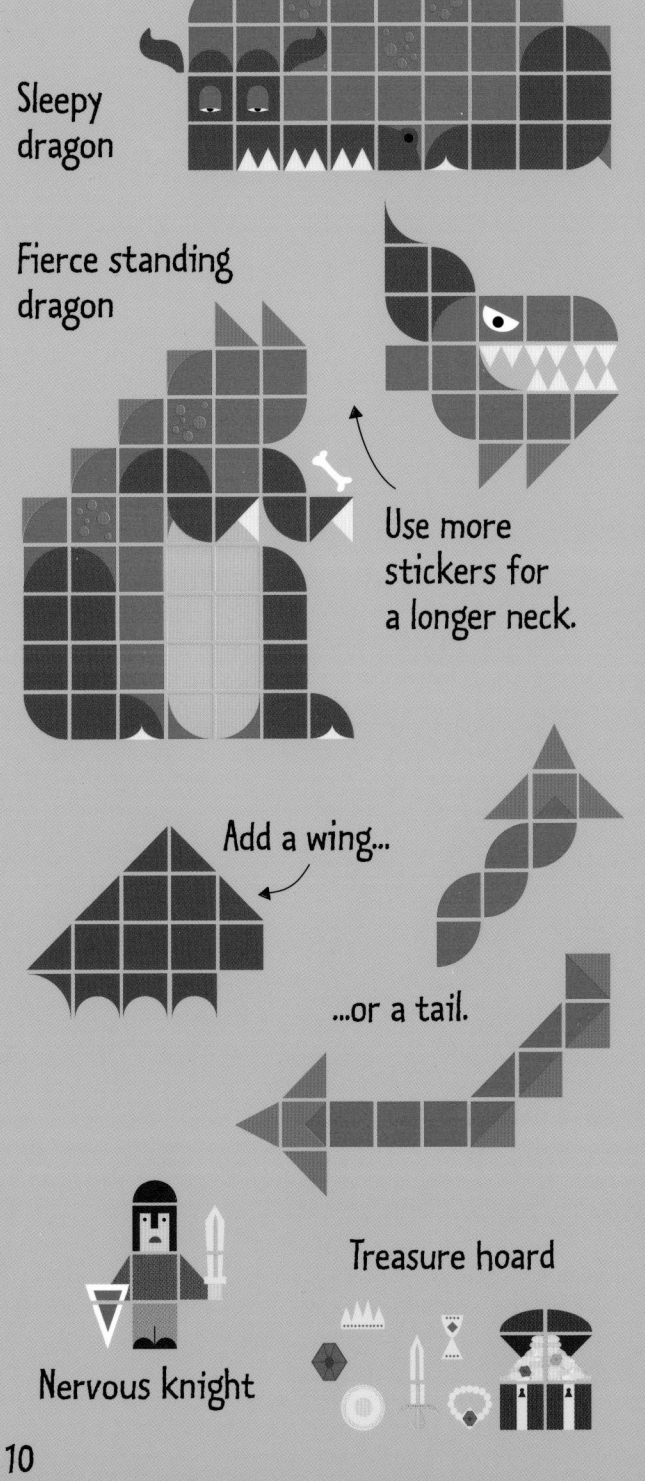

Sleepy dragon

Fierce standing dragon

Use more stickers for a longer neck.

Add a wing...

...or a tail.

Nervous knight

Treasure hoard

The outer courtyard

Below are some pictures you could make to show what's happening in the courtyard.

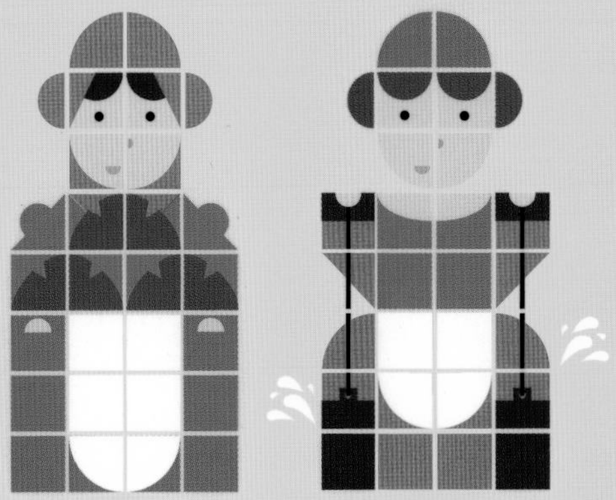

Eggs in a basket

Servants carrying bread and water

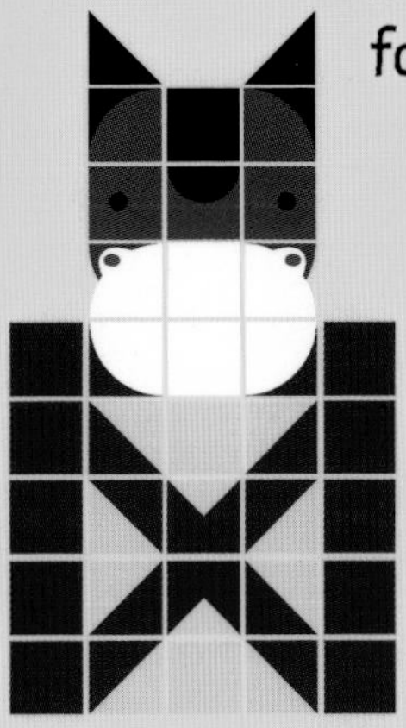

A horse waiting for new shoes

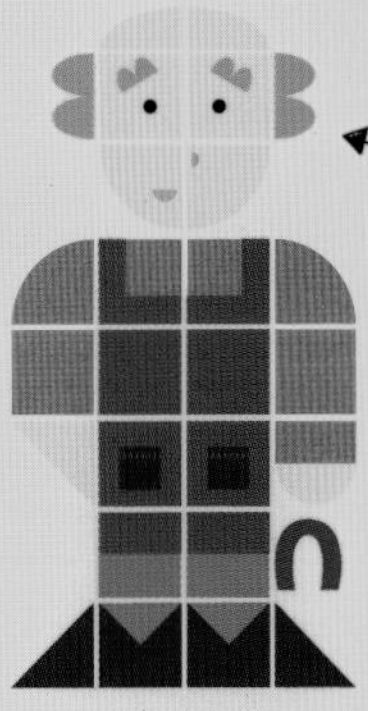

Blacksmith

Hen

Goose

A puppet show

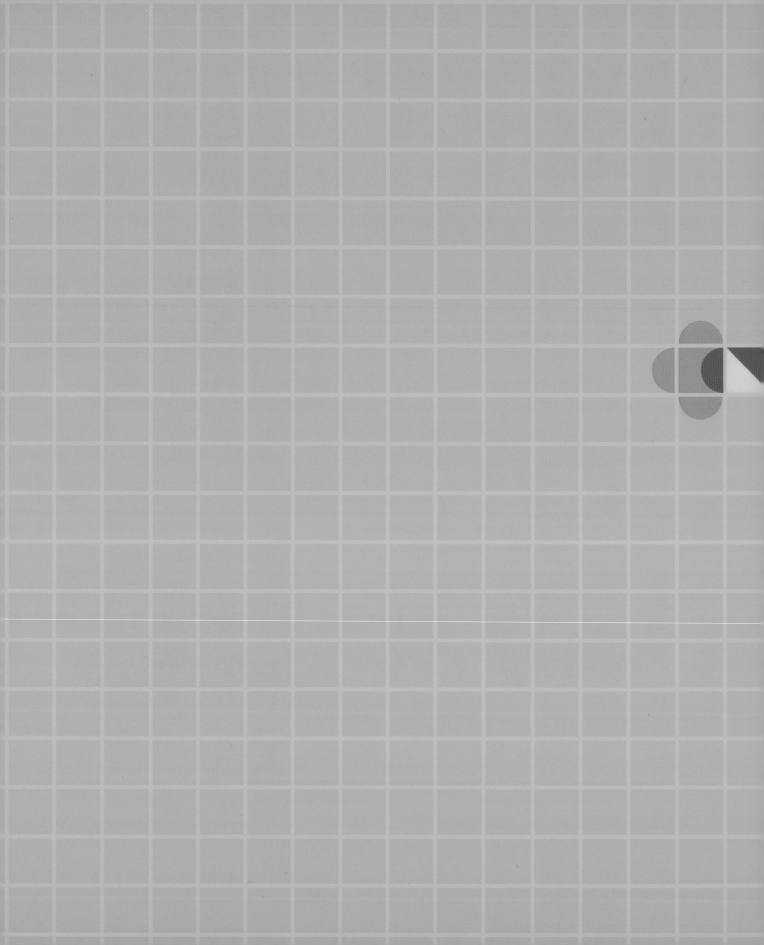

Tournament time

Use the stickers to show Sir Donald the Dark ready to face his foe.

Sturdy lance

Finish the scene with tents and flags.

Shield

Brave Sir Brian's tent has a different pattern.

Add smaller tents in the distance.

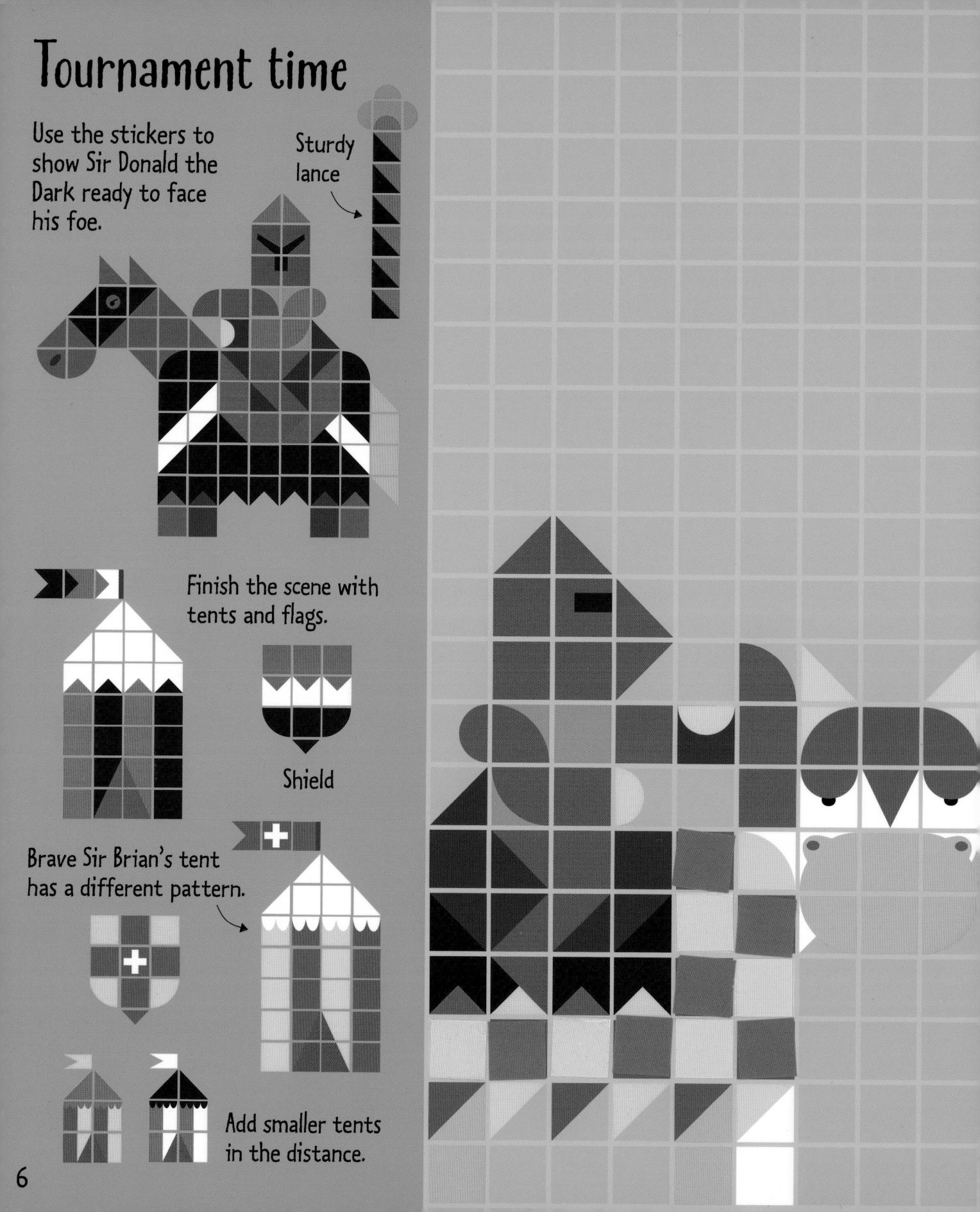

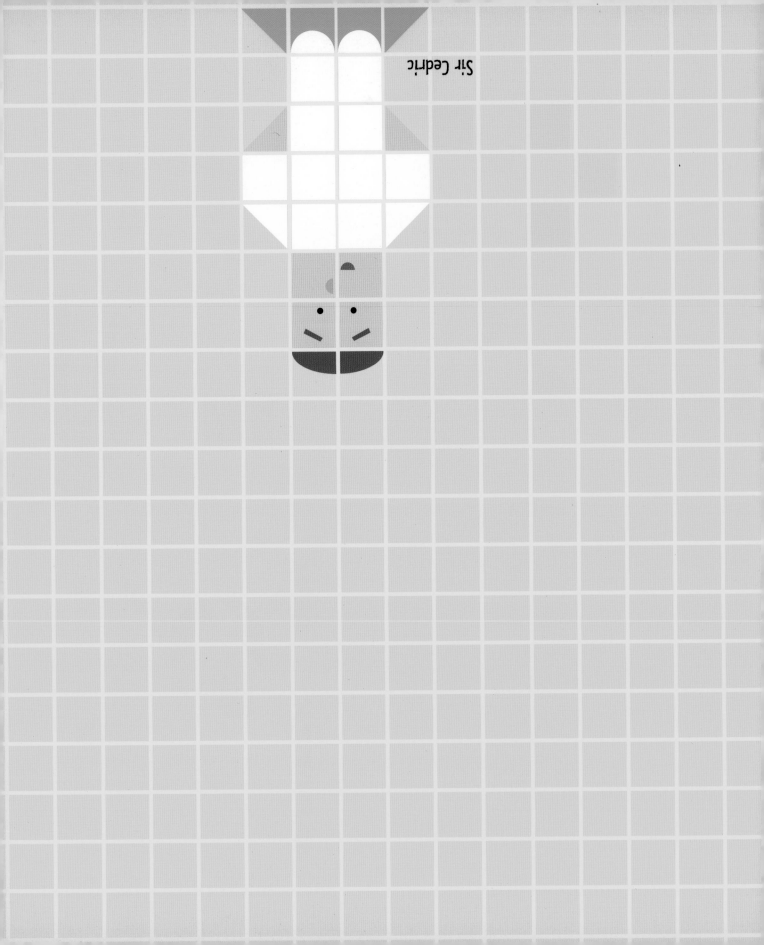

Sir Cedric

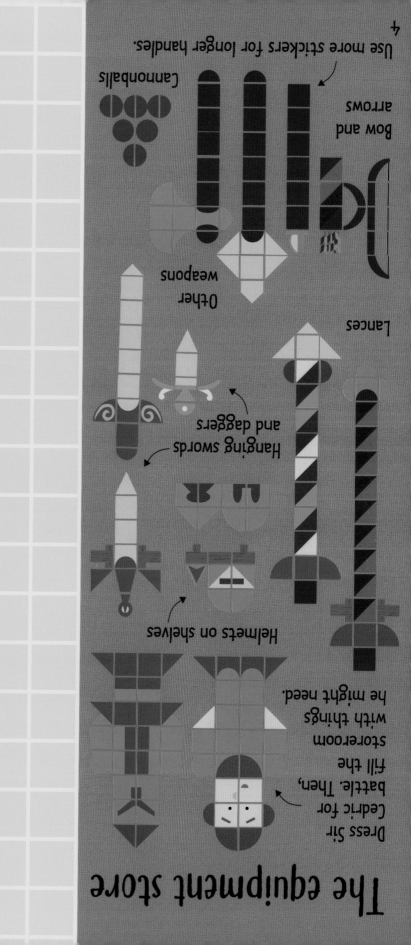

The equipment store

Dress Sir Cedric for battle. Then, fill the storeroom with things he might need.

Helmets on shelves

Hanging swords and daggers

Other weapons

Lances

Bow and arrows

Cannonballs

Use more stickers for longer handles.